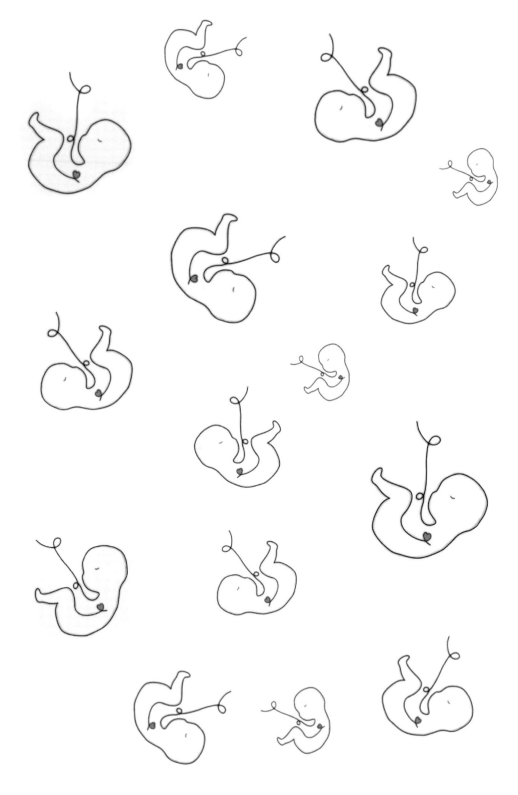

To all the beautiful pregnant women.
Pregnancy is hard but so worth it!
Trust in your body's ability to grow, birth
and nurture your baby!

Hello, Sweet Baby!

Written and Illustrated by
Lisa McArthur-Collins

First Printing, 2023

Published by Little Wings Publishing
www.littlewingspublishing.com

ABN 31 448 359 874

ISBN 978-0-6486066-0-4 Paperback version
ISBN 978-0-6486066-5-9 Hardcover version
ISBN 978-0-6486066-1-1 eBook version

Hello, Sweet Baby!

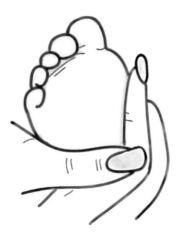

Written and Illustrated by
Lisa McArthur-Collins

Dear little one,
I hope you can hear me,
sweet baby,
as I read this to you.

I want you to know
how special you are,
and how much love
I have for you!

Every day, you're growing
bigger and stronger.

Can you feel the warmth of the hugs
and kisses I give to you?

I'm amazed when I feel you
kick and move about,
all snug inside;
I hope you haven't run out of room.

As I gently sway with you,
I dream of your future and the
person you'll be.

I want you to know my voice and feel
safe and loved when you hear it.

Preparing for your arrival is
keeping me very busy.

I want everything to be perfect...

Because I'm so excited to
hold you close!

To be there for you day and night.

So, I'm creating a special
place for you.

I have decorated it with love.

You'll have a cosy bed,
soft clothes to wear,
and a special friend to keep
you company.

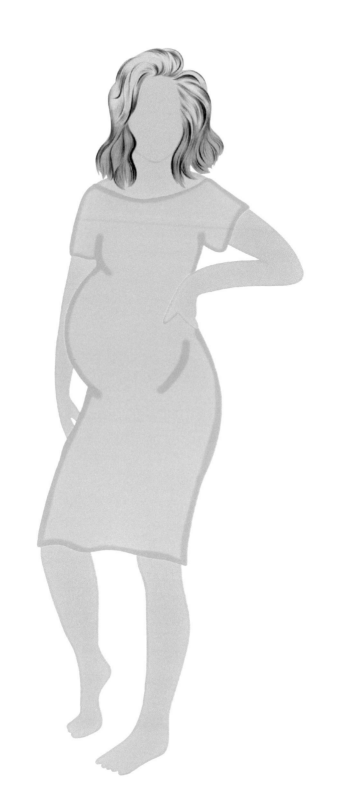

I love the bond we already share
as I sing to you a soothing sound.

I just can't wait to take you on
adventures.

To show you the world outside
waiting for you!

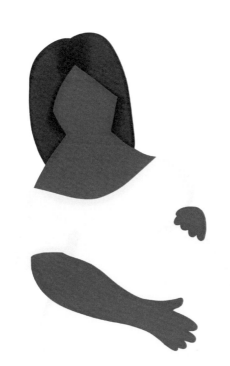

I'm getting more excited as the weeks pass by.

I'm counting down.

The day is getting closer.

Soon, I'll get to hold you in my arms.

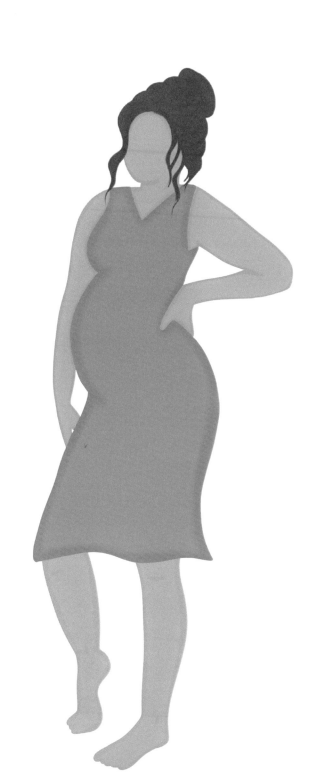

Birthing classes are fun.

They teach us how to stay
calm and positive;

A toolkit full of beautiful ways
to breathe you into
this world.

A hospital bag is being packed.

What will you need?

How many outfits do we bring?

What colour will match your eyes?

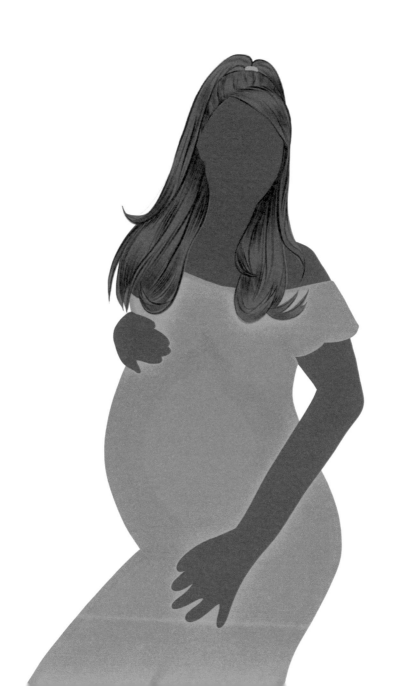

Choosing a perfect name
is harder than I thought.

I whisper some just to hear
how they sound.

Your little nicknames will
be so adorable.

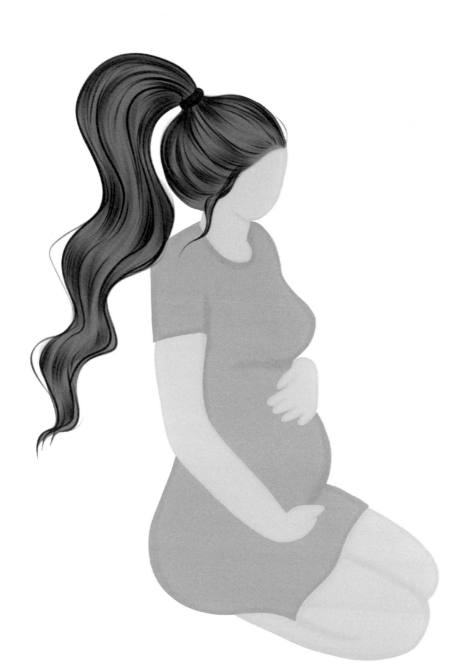

You're already showered
with gifts from loved ones.

The anticipation is growing,
the day will soon be here.

Then I can hold you close
and whisper…

"Hello there,
my sweet baby!"

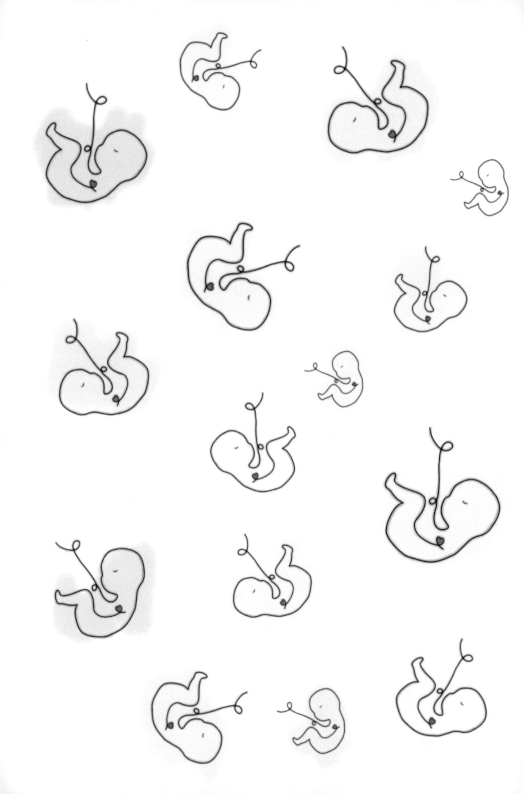

My name is Jessica,
I'm a Registered Midwife,
and I run Breathe Life Childbirth Education.
I believe birth is one of the most important events
in a woman's life.
It is your transition to motherhood.
The day you meet your baby for the first time.
Every mother deserves to be able to look back
on this day with love and joy.
Birth does not need to be something you fear
but something you can look forward to
with confidence.

You can find out more information about
the birth classes I teach on
my website.

www.breathelife.au

BREATHE LIFE
Childbirth Education

Milton Keynes UK
Ingram Content Group UK Ltd.
UKRC030100170124
436163UK00005B/30